A New England Village

In Memory

TO MY BELOVED FATHER, Arnold Deutsch, a hero who fought with the resistance in the Warsaw Ghetto uprising against Nazi tyranny. Surviving the uprising, he perished in a Treblinka gas chamber, victim of the Holocaust, in 1943. He fought and died for the dignity of man and for freedom against barbarism. He has no grave where I can lay a flower in remembrance and gratitude; therefore I dedicate this book to him, the flower of my own artistic struggle.

A New England Village

Written and Illustrated

by Eva Deutsch Costabel

ATHENEUM   1983   NEW YORK

ACKNOWLEDGMENTS

Many thanks to Dr. Jack Larkin, Chief Historian at Sturbridge Village, Massachusetts,
for taking time from his busy schedule to talk with me and to check the manuscript and artwork for historical accuracy.
Thanks also to Atheneum Publishers, especially to Marcia Marshall, my editor, and Mary Ahern, Art Director,
for helping to see my project on its way.

LIBRARY OF CONGRESS CATALOGING IN PUBLICATION DATA

Costabel, Eva Deutsch   New England village.

Bibliography: p. 42.
SUMMARY: Describes life in a New England village of about 1830,
emphasizing household and village crafts such as candlemaking, quilting, weaving, printing, and tinsmithing.
1. City and town life—New England—History—19th century—Juvenile literature.
2. New England—Social life and customs—Juvenile literature.
[1. City and town life—New England.
2. New England—Social life and customs.   3. Handicraft—New England]   I. Title.
F8.C84   1983   974'.03   82-13738
ISBN 0-689-30972-4

Text and pictures copyright © 1982, 1983 by Eva Deutsch Costabel
All rights reserved
Published simultaneously in Canada by McClelland & Stewart, Ltd.
Composition by Dix Type, Inc., Syracuse, New York
Printed and bound by The Halliday Lithograph Corporation, West Hanover, Massachusetts
Title on the jacket and the title page calligraphed by Anita Karl
Designed by Mary Ahern and Eva Deutsch Costabel
First Edition

CONTENTS

Introduction

I WROTE AND ILLUSTRATED THIS BOOK with the hope of recreating, as closely and convincingly as possible, life in a New England town one hundred and fifty years ago. I wanted to convey the thrill I felt as a European when I first saw the old houses with their lovely interiors and their handsome hand-crafted housewares. The settlers had brought with them their English heritage, but they had had to change it to meet the demands of a new land. They built their first homes in a wilderness with a few hand tools, and what they lacked in equipment they made up for in imagination.

The early settlers had to work hard, use their ingenuity and develop a team spirit within the family and with their neighbors. These traits formed the American heritage. By learning more about how our ancestors in America lived and worked, we can come to truly treasure this heritage that has come down to us.

And now I would like to invite you to visit with me one of the typical towns of the New England of one hundred and fifty years ago; to enter the homes and shops and walk the quiet roads, reliving our American past.

Eva Deutsch Costabel

1

THE HOUSE

The early New England houses were made of wood. Oak was used a great deal for the basic frame of the house, pine in the exterior siding. Wooden shingles covered the roof, too, but by the 1830s, iron nails were being used widely in place of the wooden pegs of the past.

The man who built a house was called a housewright and he was a master craftsman with a good practical knowledge of construction and architecture. Many small houses were built by their owners a room at a time, or neighbors would join together for a house-raising. A poor family might have a one-room house with only a few small windows, because glass was expensive. Then as they prospered they might add a lean-to addition along the back. A wealthy family would have a full two-story house with a parlor, bedchambers and dining room.

THE FARM KITCHEN

The kitchen was the most important room of the house. Food was cooked over the open fire and meals were often eaten in the kitchen. There the housewife prepared the meals, churned butter, made cheese and preserved food. Dinner was eaten around noon, tea served about four o'clock and supper between six and eight.

Most housekeeping chores were done in the kitchen in the winter, the one room where there was always a warm fire. The farm wife or the grandmother, if she lived with them, might rock the baby in its cradle while she peeled and sliced apples for drying or pie. A daughter might knit mittens or card wool, and the schoolchildren did their lessons at the kitchen table. In the evening father had harnesses to mend, tools to fix or account books to keep, and the mother always had darning, mending and knitting to fill in her evening hours.

THE BEDCHAMBER

The bedchamber, the term New Englanders used, might be a bedroom for the whole family until there was time and money to build extra rooms; or older children might have a room in the loft, the space above the first floor and below the roof. The baby's cradle might be moved to the parents' room at night, although often the baby slept with its mother and father for warmth and to make night feedings easier.

Bedrooms weren't heated, so quilts or wool blankets were necessary for much of the year. To make getting into bed more pleasant, a bedwarmer, a warmed stone or brick wrapped in cloth or a pan filled with hot coals, was run over the bottom sheet to take out the dampness and cold.

CANDLEMAKING

One of the many tasks one hundred and fifty years ago was candlemaking. Most candles were made from tallow, which comes from beef and sheep fat, so candles were usually made once a year after the animals were slaughtered.

The fat was melted in water in a large kettle and the hard bits, the tallow, skimmed off. Tallow candles smelled of animal fat and tended to sag in hot weather.

The candles were usually made by dipping, but could also be formed in candle molds. In the dipping method, the string wicks were dipped over and over again into the hot tallow until the layers of tallow formed a candle of the proper thickness. Candle molds, usually made of tin, were threaded with the string wicks and the hot tallow was poured into each of the openings. It usually took about two days to make enough candles for a year.

QUILTING

The patchwork quilt was welcome in the drafty houses and unheated bedrooms of early America. Although by 1830 handwoven wool blankets were more popular, making quilts remained an occasional pastime.

Women collected scraps of fabric for their quilts, and when they had enough they worked in their spare time, fitting the bits of cloth into patterned squares or sewing one kind on another in an appliqué design. After the squares were stitched together to make the patterned top, this, the center padding, and a plain or printed bottom cover were stretched on a quilting frame, and the three layers sewn together in a series of simple knots or in a more elaborate all-over design of small stitches.

Although a woman often quilted alone or with one or two friends, a quilting bee might be organized. Then a group of women worked together around the quilting frame, exchanging gossip and news. Or one might read the Bible aloud while the others worked and the children played with their friends. If young women were at the bee, young men might come later in the evening for courting.

SPINNING, WEAVING AND DYEING

In an earlier time in New England, the housewife had to make linen from flax, as well as wool yarn for the family's clothing, but by the 1830s, cotton fabric was being manufactured in many places.

Most farmers did keep a few sheep for wool. The sheep were sheared in the spring and the fleece was carded with special brushes to straighten the fibers or put through a special carding mill. The fibers were dyed and then spun into yarn on a spinning wheel. The housewife took pride in coloring her yarns and grew a variety of plants for use as dyes. Butternut hulls gave a strong brown color; madder root, reds and browns; onion skins made yellow; sumac produced beige; and indigo, obtained from a variety of plants, was used for blue.

Often weaving was done at home, though someone in town might specialize in this craft and weave for those who brought them wool. A large loom was set up in the house and fabric for clothing was made, as well as blankets in many patterns and reversible wool and cotton coverlets.

THE GARDEN

Every farmhouse had its own garden divided into three parts. The flower garden was usually in front of the house and provided beauty with such flowers and shrubs as lilac, calendula, peonies and lilies. There was also an orchard of apple, pear and cherry trees and many sorts of berry bushes.

The vegetable garden was usually behind the house, and the New England housewife grew a great many different vegetables: beans, peas, cabbage, lettuce, radishes, turnips, beets, and onions.

Many kinds of herbs for cooking, for medicine and for dyes were also grown, including garlic, rosemary, sweet basil, winter savory, thyme, chives, parsley, mustard, peppermint, camomile and lavender. The herbs were dried to be used all through the year.

THE FARM

The New England farm of the early nineteenth century was a very busy place. Every member of the family had to contribute to the work, even children of six and seven. In the spring, summer and fall the farm day was long. The family would rise with the sun to care for the livestock, and in the spring they had to prepare the fields for planting the corn and rye and other crops. During the summer the fields had to be hoed and weeded, and the ripened grain harvested and threshed. When the corn was harvested, neighbors "changed work," and gathered at each house in turn for husking bees to husk the corn for winter use as flour and feed.

The New England farmer raised many kinds of livestock for meat. Cattle also provided milk; pigs leather and bristles; sheep gave wool; and chickens, turkeys and geese, eggs, and feathers for pillows and featherbeds. A pair of oxen was kept to pull the plow and the farm wagon. In spring and summer cattle and sheep could graze in the pastures, but hay had to be cut and stored in the hayloft of the barn to feed the animals during the winter months.

THE TOWN AND THE VILLAGE

In 1830, the boundaries of a New England town might enclose thirty or so square miles. In this area there would be about one hundred farms and two to three small villages of five to thirty houses.

As soon as a group of families settled in an area, a church and school were established and the people organized a local government. In the early days of the nineteenth century most New Englanders were likely to be Congregationalists, a Protestant church in which all of the members governed the church. By 1830, there might also be a Methodist or Baptist church as well. The town settled its problems, established its laws and chose its selectmen at a town meeting of all eligible voters, though at that time, only men who owned property were allowed to vote.

By this time most towns in the southern part of New England had been settled for one hundred years or more. There was a good deal of travel and trade between towns and villages all over New England and the first textile mills and railroads had been built. New England, then, was entering the modern era.

THE DISTRICT SCHOOL

The district school of about one hundred and fifty years ago was a simple, one-room structure with straight wooden benches. In the winter the schoolhouse was heated by a wood stove, and firewood was supplied by the parents of the school children. By law, each town had to provide schooling, but parents weren't forced to send their children.

Teachers didn't need a special education to teach and it was hard to find good teachers, especially as the salary was low. The teacher often boarded with one of the families in town as part of his or her wages.

There was no grading in the nineteenth century school. Students in the classroom were different ages, and it was not unusual to find one child studying the alphabet, while the older ones were preparing for an academy or college. Most children went to school only until their early or mid-teens, then went to work full time on the family farm, or were apprenticed to a craftsman. Those who were eager for more education might continue at a private academy in a larger town or go on to one of the handful of colleges of the time.

THE GRISTMILL

Each settlement had a gristmill to make flour from the grains the settlers grew. The mill was built near a stream so that the energy of the flowing water rushing over the water wheel turned it and, through a series of gears, the giant grinding stones. Often a dam was constructed to create a waterfall to provide still more water power.

A variety of grains were ground in the mill. Corn was a staple the early settlers learned to grow from the Native Americans. Wheat was scarce then because it was subject to blights, but the New Englanders did grow rye, and the most common flour of the day was a mixture of corn and rye, used to bake a loaf called Indian bread.

THE GENERAL STORE

The country store was filled with wares to satisfy the needs and wants of most people because, by 1830, a wide variety of goods from all over the world was available to the rural community. The store shelves were filled with such foods as loaf sugar, tea, coffee, chocolate, pepper, salt, molasses, rice, raisins, figs, salt cod and herring. There might also be Madeira wine and West Indian rum. In the spring the store carried a good selection of garden seed, which the Shaker communities packaged and sold.

Children could choose a stick of penny candy. Their mothers could select a new bonnet, woolen shawl or dress fabric from the bolts of the newest cotton prints. The farmer might buy an axe or scythe, a whetstone or hat. A family could bring vegetables, meats, butter and eggs in trade.

The store stocked tinplate utensils, coffeepots and teapots, a variety of lamps, blue-edged plates from England, painted tinware, shoes, ribbons and hardware.

THE BLACKSMITH

The blacksmith was one of the most important craftsmen in an agricultural community. He worked molten iron by heating it in a furnace and hammering it on an anvil to produce many items for the farm, including plows, hoes, pitchforks and axes. The smith also made horse bits and hinges and iron wheel rims for farm wagons and carriages. He made locks and keys, door hinges and other iron items for the home, such as hooks and chains and some cutlery.

By 1830, many of these things were being manufactured in foundries and sold in the general store, though the blacksmith might be called on to sharpen or repair them.

Another important job of the blacksmith continued well into this century, for he made and fitted the iron shoes worn by horses and oxen to protect their feet. He is likely to be best remembered today for this work.

THE PRINTING OFFICE

The rural printer might publish a newspaper and print pamphlets and books, but he also produced legal forms, handbills, calling cards and other printing people might need. He was not only a printing craftsman, but a newspaper and book editor and publisher.

The printer put together type made of single, raised-metal letters to form the words and lines of the text. This was printed on a large, hand-run press in the process known as letterpress printing.

To learn this craft, a boy might apprentice to a master printer who might even be his father. Once he was fully trained, he was called a journeyman and might travel from printshop to printshop learning more skills before he opened his own shop.

THE POTTER'S CRAFT

Pottery, in the form of crocks, jugs, plates, pitchers, milkpans and flowerpots was essential to the early American home. Jugs were used as containers for liquids, such as vinegar and molasses, the crocks stored grains and flours, and preserved foods. To practice his craft, the potter needed a potter's wheel, a mill for grinding clay and one for grinding glazes, a large brick furnace called a kiln for firing, and a supply of clay.

The most popular early pottery in New England was redware, made from the local clays available near streams and ponds and at the seashore. The clay was cleaned of stones and other impurities, dried and ground, then mixed with water to the proper consistency. Most shapes were formed by the potter on his wheel, then baked in the kiln, which was heated to high temperatures. Decorations and glaze, to make the surface less porous, were usually made from powdered lead sifted over the surface before firing. Later people complained of the lead, which could cause poisoning, and the stoneware process, begun in Germany, became more popular. The stoneware, fired at higher temperatures with a different kind of clay, makes a harder pottery, glazed by throwing salt into the kiln during firing.

THE TINSMITH

Tinsmithing required only a few basic tools: a large pair of shears, a soldering iron, a mallet and iron wire for soldering. Tinplate was made by dipping thin sheets of cast iron into molten tin. The more the iron was dipped, the more durable the product became.

There was a great demand for tinplate items, since tinware was shiny, easy to clean, lightweight and didn't break. It was a welcome change from heavy wooden pails, pewter, which, with its lead content, could be poisonous, and fragile pottery. Many useful household objects were made of tinplate, such as teapots, coffeepots, lanterns with perforated designs, candlesticks, trays, molds, pails and pots and pans. The pattern for the object was cut from the tinplate, then bent into shape and the edges soldered together. Decorative tinware items painted black with bright-colored designs were sold in the general store and also created at home.

THE SHOE SHOP

In the early days, it was quite customary for the man of the house to make shoes for the whole family. But by 1830, people wanted to wear the more comfortable, less crudely-made shoes that were being sold at the local store. These shoes were of soft leather and in the same shape for each foot.

Because there was such a demand for "ready made" shoes, the local trained shoemaker worked out the beginnings of what is now called mass production. He hired and trained men, women and children to stitch together the various parts of the shoes from leather he cut out and supplied. This was a cottage industry, because the workers worked at home either full time or between regular farm tasks. The workers were paid on a "piecework basis," that is, for each piece finished rather than by the hour. The stitched pieces were delivered to the shoemaker for finishing and distribution to the local stores.

THE TAVERN

In the early days Americans traveled from place to place on horses or in stagecoaches, over rough, rutted and often muddy roads. The interiors of the coaches were cramped, and the iron-rimmed wooden wheels did nothing to soften the bumps in the road. To help travelers on their way, taverns sprang up along the route offering food and rest for the journeyers and their horses.

The tavern not only provided food, drink and beds to guests, but also a place for local people and travelers to meet and talk. Rooms were never reserved in advance because, in a time when travel was difficult, it was expected that no one would be turned away, even if it meant more people in each bed.

The barroom, where hard cider and liquors such as rum and gin were served to the local people, as well as overnight guests, was usually on the first floor. There was often also a parlor, where guests ate together and would spend the evening exchanging news of various parts of the country, reading newspapers, or playing cards and other games before going to bed.

THE COVERED BRIDGE

It is hard to picture an early New England landscape without seeing in it a covered bridge. The main function of the bridge's roof was to protect the timbers from bad weather, but it also might protect a traveler from an unexpected downpour or snowstorm and give relief from the hot sun. Advertisers also took advantage of this protection to hang their posters out of the weather, and children found the bridges a good place to play.

Some bridges had latticed sides to let in sunlight and prevent dark places where robbers might lurk. Others were fully sided, with windows to let in the light. Some were single lane and others provided for two-way traffic. Fire was the greatest enemy of the wooden bridges, and there were strict rules prohibiting smoking by those passing through.

Bibliography

America's Arts and Skills, by the editors of *Life*. E. P. Dutton & Co., Inc., New York.

Black, Mary and Lipman, Jean. *American Folk Painting*. Bramhall House, New York.

Chamberlain, Samuel. *A Tour of Old Sturbridge Village*. Hastings House, New York.

Copeland, F. *Early American Trades Coloring Book*. Dover Publications, New York.

Davidson, Marshall B. *Three Centuries of American Antiques*. American Heritage Publishing Co., Inc.

Dolan, J. R. *The Yankee Peddlers of Early America*. Clarkson N. Potter, Inc., New York.

Favretti, Rudy J. *Early New England Garden*. Old Sturbridge Village, Sturbridge, Massachusetts.

Fennelly, Catherine. *New England Character*. Old Sturbridge Village, Sturbridge, Massachusetts.

————. *Town Schooling in Early New England*. Old Sturbridge Village, Sturbridge, Massachusetts.

Folk Arts and Crafts of New England, The. Chilton Book Company, Philadelphia.

Hamilton, Edward P. *The Village Mill in Early New England*. Old Sturbridge Village, Sturbridge, Massachusetts.

Hornung, Clarence P. *Treasury of American Design*. Harry N. Abrams, Inc., Publishers, New York.

Lipman, Jean, and Winchester, Alice. *American Folk Art*. The Viking Press, New York, in cooperation with the Whitney Museum of American Art.

Stears, Martha Genung. *Herbs and Herb Cookery through the Years*. Old Sturbridge Village, Sturbridge, Massachusetts.

Van Wagenen, Jared, Jr. *The Golden Age of Homespun*. Hill and Wang, New York.

Watkins, Lura Woodside. *Early New England Pottery*. Old Sturbridge Village, Sturbridge, Massachusetts.

HHT   93 96 98 0e
       1   1   1

NO RENEWALS!

PLEASE RETURN BOOK AND REQUEST
AGAIN.